Melania Trump

First Lady & Be Best Backer

by Grace Hansen

Abdo

HISTORY MAKER
BIOGRAPHIES

Kids

AUG 20

abdobooks.com

Published by Abdo Kids, a division of ABDO, P.O. Box 398166, Minneapolis, Minnesota 55439.
Copyright © 2020 by Abdo Consulting Group, Inc. International copyrights reserved in all countries.
No part of this book may be reproduced in any form without written permission from the publisher.
Abdo Kids Jumbo™ is a trademark and logo of Abdo Kids.

Printed in the United States of America, North Mankato, Minnesota.

102019

012020

THIS BOOK CONTAINS
RECYCLED MATERIALS

Photo Credits: Alamy, AP Images, Getty Images, iStock, newscom, Shutterstock,
©Shutterstock PREMIER p.17

Production Contributors: Teddy Borth, Jennie Forsberg, Grace Hansen
Design Contributors: Dorothy Toth, Pakou Moua

Library of Congress Control Number: 2019941250

Publisher's Cataloging-in-Publication Data

Names: Hansen, Grace, author.

Title: Melania Trump / by Grace Hansen

Other title: First lady & be best backer

Description: Minneapolis, Minnesota : Abdo Kids, 2020 | Series: History maker biographies | Includes
    online resources and index.

Identifiers: ISBN 9781532189012 (lib. bdg.) | ISBN 9781532189500 (ebook) | ISBN 9781098200480
    (Read-to-Me ebook)

Subjects: LCSH: Trump, Melania, 1970---Juvenile literature. | Fashion models--Biography--Juvenile
    literature. | Presidents' spouses--United States--Biography--Juvenile literature. | Women entrepreneurs--
    Biography--Juvenile literature. | First ladies--Biography--Juvenile literature.

Classification: DDC 973.93309 [B]--dc23

Table of Contents

Early Years

Melanija Knavs was born on April 26, 1970 in present-day Slovenia. She grew up in a town called Sevnica. She would later change her name to Melania Knauss.

Asia

Europe

Slovenia

Africa

5

Her father sold cars. Her mother worked in a **textile** factory that made children's clothes. Young Melania modeled the clothes.

In 1992, Melania left university to model. She had come in second place in a contest with the Slovenian magazine, *Jana*. She won a modeling **contract** that would take her to Milan, Italy.

Slovenia

Italy

9

In 1996, she signed with a new **modeling agency**. This one was in New York City, New York!

Europe

New York City
1996

Melania attended a party in 1998. There she met Donald Trump. He was a well-known businessman. The two married in 2005. They welcomed their son Barron in 2006.

13

Becoming First Lady

In June 2015, Donald Trump announced his run for president. He won the election in November 2016. In January 2017, Melania became the First Lady of the United States.

14

15

Be Best

Before Trump was sworn into office, Melania knew what she wanted to do as First Lady. She would work to prevent **cyberbullying**. She also wanted to help stop bullying in schools.

In May 2018, Melania launched her Be Best campaign. It focuses on the well-being of children in the United States.

19

In October of 2018, Melania brought Be Best abroad. She went to many countries in Africa. While there she visited schools and **orphanages**. Her goal was for "children around the world to live a beautiful life, to be safe and secure."

Timeline

Melania begins her modeling career.

Melania meets future husband Donald Trump.

Melania becomes First Lady of the United States.

Melania takes her first trip to Africa to visit schools, hospitals, and shelters that care for children.

1986

1998

2017

2018

1970

1996

2005

2018

Melanija Knavs is born in Slovenia.

Melania moves to New York City to continue her modeling career.

Melania marries Donald and a year later they welcome their son Barron.

Melania announces her platform Be Best. It focuses on the well-being of the nation's children.

Glossary

contract – an agreement that is supported by the law.

cyberbullying – bullying that is done by posting hurtful electronic messages on the internet.

modeling agency – a company that represents fashion models to work for the fashion industry.

orphanage – a place where orphans live and are cared for.

textile – having to do with weaving or making fabric.

Index

Abdo Kids
ONLINE
FREE! ONLINE MULTIMEDIA RESOURCES

Visit **abdokids.com**
to access crafts, games,
videos, and more!

Use Abdo Kids code
HMK9012
or scan this QR code!